The Old Liberators

NEW AND SELECTED
POEMS AND TRANSLATIONS

The Old Liberators

NEW AND SELECTED
POEMS AND TRANSLATIONS

Robert Hedin

ARTWORK BY PERRY INGLI

HOLY COW! PRESS · DULUTH, MINNESOTA · 1998

This project is supported, in part, by a grant from the Arrowhead Regional Arts Council through an appropriation from the Minnesota State Legislature, and by generous individuals.

Library of Congress Cataloging-in-Publication Data

Hedin, Robert, 1949-
    The old liberators : new and selected poems and translations / by Robert Hedin.
        p. cm.
    English, with some translated selections from the Norwegian poet Rolf Jacobsen.
    ISBN 0-930100-81-6 (cloth). — ISBN 0-930100-80-8 (paper)
    1. Jacobsen, Rolf—Translations into English.   I. Jacobsen. Rolf.
    II. Title.
    PS3558.E318043   1998
    811' . 54—dc21   98-2601
                                                                            CIP

Holy Cow! Press books are distributed to the trade by Consortium Book Sales & Distribution, 1045 Westgate Drive, Saint Paul, Minnesota 55114. Our books are available through all major library distributors and jobbers, and through most small press distributors, including Bookpeople and Small Press Distribution. For personal orders, catalogs or other information, write to: Holy Cow! Press
        Post Office Box 3170
        Mount Royal Station
        Duluth, Minnesota 55803

Some of these poems and translations have previously appeared in the following publications, to whose editors grateful acknowledgement is made: *Alaska Quarterly Review, Beloit Poetry Journal, Carolina Quarterly, Chariton Review, Chowder Review, Colorado Review, Copperhead, Cutbank, Dacotah Territory, Epoch, Fiddlehead* (Can.), *Free Passage, Georgia State Review, Great Circumpolar Bear Cult, Great River Review, Greenfield Review, Greensboro Review, International Poetry Review, Iron* (UK), *Kansas Quarterly, Literary Review, Malahat Review* (Can.), *Mankato Poetry Review, Mid-American Review, Minnesota Monthly, Missouri Review, Montana Review, Nebraska Review, Nimrod, North Coast Review, Pembroke Magazine, Permafrost, Poetry, Poetry East, Poetry Ireland Review, Poetry Now, Poetry Review* (UK), *Poetry Wales, Porch, Portland Review, Prism International* (Can.), *Puerto Del Sol, Raccoon, Scarp Australia, Seattle Review, Southern Poetry Review, Sou'wester, Three Rivers Poetry Journal, Wascana Review* (Can.), and *Willow Springs.*

Anthology of Magazine Verse and Yearbook of American Poetry, ed. Alan Pater (Monitor Book Co., 1991, 1988, 1986, 1981); *Articulations: The Body and Illness in Poetry,* ed. Jon Mukand (University of Iowa Press, 1994); *Cardinal: A Contemporary Anthology of North Carolina Writers,* ed. Richard Krawiec (Jacar Press, 1984); *The Gift of Tongues: Twenty-Five Years of Poetry from Copper Canyon Press,* ed. Sam Hamill (Copper Canyon Press, 1996); *Rain in the Forest/Light in the Trees: Contemporary Poetry from the Northwest,* ed. Rich Ives (Owl Creek Press, 1984); *Season of Dead Water,* ed. Helen Frost (Breitenbush, 1990); and *Windflower Anthology of Poetry,* ed. Ted Kooser (Windflower Press, 1983).

The author also wishes to thank the following publishers for permission to reprint poems and translations which previously appeared in broadside, pamphlet or book: Copper Canyon Press; Ion Books, Inc.; Jawbone Press; Mad River Press; Old Harbor Press; Ox Head Press; and State Street Press.

Grateful acknowledgement is made to the National Endowment for the Arts, the Bush Foundation, the Minnesota State Arts Board, the North Carolina State Arts Council, and the Corporation of Yaddo for their assistance, financial or otherwise, during the writing and translating of many of these poems.

Contents

Preface

The poems and translations collected in *The Old Liberators* have been selected from twenty-five years of work. Many of the poems are presented as they were first written and as they were originally published in books, chapbooks, pamphlets, and broadsides. In some cases, I have recast particular lines, have deleted or added stanzas, or have altered certain titles. In other cases, I have completely redrafted poems that were not entirely satisfying to me at the time of their original publication. "White Out," for example, a poem first written in the mid 1970s, was a substantially longer poem; the version presented here is dramatically different in both length and tone, and for all intents and purposes it is a brand new poem.

I have also sought out new sequences for the poems in the volume. Poems that were conceived months or even years apart from each other have been placed side by side in hopes that together they shed a fuller, more meaningful light upon their subjects. Both "Waiting for Trains at Col d'Aubisque" and "At the Blessing of the Children in Lourdes," for instance, were written at decidedly different periods in my life. One was written in the late 1970s while I was living in France, the other more than a decade later after I had returned to the United States and was living in North Carolina. The same can be said for the five poems entitled "Tornado" that comprise the bulk of the last section of the book. They were all written at different times and locations, and under different circumstances. In arranging the poems as I have done, I have felt no particular allegiance to the chronological order of their composition nor to their arrangements in earlier volumes. Instead, they are presented here in ways that stress certain sympathies and preoccupations, themes and sensibilities, that have sometimes taken years to emerge.

In many ways, the poems and translations in *The Old Liberators* represent a kind of journey, one that has taken place over a long period of time as well as over a wide expanse of geography. There are poems of Alaska, France, Germany, and North Africa. There are also poems that deal with the Mississippi River and the Minnesota farmlands, places that I knew as a child and ones that I have come to know again as an adult. I have also included a number of translations of the poetry of Rolf Jacobsen, the distinguished Norwegian modernist whose work I have translated on and off for the last ten years. The translations reveal Jacobsen's themes of modern alienation, his subtle and wry voice, as well as his remarkable ability to recover some of the original grandeur and mystery of the universe.

Although the subjects, styles, and settings may vary throughout the book, the main concerns of my poems remain consistent: home and home-ground, loss and reclamation, the integrity of everyday events, family life, our proper place in the natural world with all its seasonal turnings and yearly migrations, and the saving grace of the individual imagination. Behind each and every one of the poems in this volume is the underlying belief that poetry, with its ability to illuminate, to sustain and confirm, is itself a kind of old liberator.

I wish to express my thanks to several people for their unfailing generosity, patience, and encouragement over the years: Jim Hans, Sam Hamill, Roberta Spear, Olga Broumas, Michael Waters, and Roger Greenwald. In addition, I wish to thank Jim Perlman, founder and editor of Holy Cow! Press, for his subtle persistence and quiet illuminations.

—*Robert Hedin*

For Carolyn

For Alex and Ben

For what was the lime engendered in our bones,
our bodies made to rise in the bright sun and
again in dust to be laid down?

Loren Eiseley

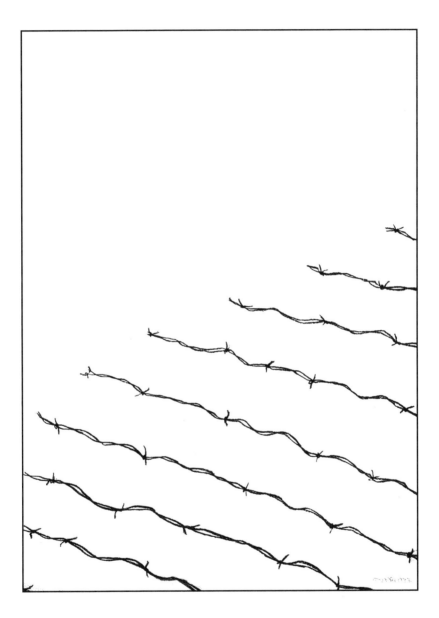

I

The Snow Country

for Carolyn

Up on Verstovia the snow country is silent tonight.
I can see it from our window,
A white sea whose tide flattens over the darkness.
This is where the animals must go—
The old foxes, the bears too slow to catch
The fall run of salmon, even the salmon themselves—
All brought together in the snow country of Verstovia.
This must be where the ravens turn to geese,
The weasels to wolves, where the rabbits turn to owls.
I wonder if birds even nest on that floating sea,
What hunters have forgotten their trails and sunk out of sight.
I wonder if the snow country is green underneath,
If there are forests and paths
And cabins with wood-burning stoves.
Or does it move down silently gyrating forever,
Glistening with the bones of animals and trappers,
Eggs that are cold and turning to stones.
I wonder if I should turn, tap, and even wake you.

Herds

On clear nights when I walk
The path back home,
I see animals glistening with frost
High in the grasslands.

Legends say they are small
Seas of breath
Stranded from an age lit by snow,
That when thaw comes

They stray through the foothills,
Leaving a strange language
Free in the streams,
Herds of lichen grazing on stones.

Goddard Hot Springs

When you lie in these sweating streams
You are lying in the breath of your ancestors,
The old pioneers who sat here in these pools
Mapping trails to the mother lode.
You feel a fog drift through your body,
A voice that is strangely familiar
And still has stories to tell.

Ancestors

for Robert Davis

The Indians on this island tell a story about fog.
They say in its belly
The spirits of the drowned are turned into otters
That on cold nights when these lowlands
Smolder with steam
The loon builds its nest in their voices.
And I remember you telling me
Of a clan of friends you had heard in a dream
All quietly singing to themselves.
Ancestors you said
People you hadn't seen in years
Each wrapped in otter
And offering a piece of last month's moon
A small amulet that glowed
In the dark like bone.
All around you could see baskets
Of berries wet with rain
And deep in the fog fish sweetening on racks.

Pilot, Drowned Young

When the night-fishermen spotted you
In the light off the jetty,
You were balled-up and bloomed,
Shimmering like a jewel.
And somehow the sea believed,
And took you in.
For days, my friend,
The fishermen talked of your spine.
They said it shone in the dark like coral.
Ted, I imagine you camped
Where that old salmon-wheel smolders
In the moonlight.
Friend of the loons,
You wear their pearls like amulets.
And I dream you are building a cockpit
Out of kelp and seaweed,
That you drift naked in the rain—
A pilot for all the salmon that come
To drown in the air.
You sing, and plunge, and bank
Into the dead calm.
And somehow the sea believes.

The Kelp-Cutters

Ten years since I buried
All the air I could,
And followed you
Down into that dark,
Seeing your breath shimmer
Like stars on the kelp.
Joe, when we broke through
That last time and found
The boat gone, the air
So cold we lay there
Not saying a word,
Hand in hand, treading
Until your warm grip went slack—
Joe, I could do nothing
But ride with the kelp
Into dawn, rocking
In the cold slate,
Listening to myself pump
The damp night full of breath.

Sitka Spruce

1.

I swear these trees come from before,
Dumb stragglers from the edge.
In their trunks the fossil worm still sings.
In the shade of each branch
There are crickets still barking like sea lions.
Legends tell of main veins shooting
Deep into the earth
To feed off pools of red lava,
That some run south along the fault lines,
Churning through coastal bays and inlets—
And when a Latin peasant clears his land
The cutting and crackling of roots
Is felt here, far north
Where a tree will shiver and shed one cone.

2.

My wife and I watch the orphan trunks
Ride with the tide back to the land.
They roll and slide like whales,
Their smooth brown backs flashing in the sun.
We have seen them drifting in the Bering—

Uncut totems beautifully round and faceless,
Waiting for the masks of ancient clans
To rise and chant again like the winds
That draw the foam from the sea.

3 .

I have heard that when we die
These spruce will take and mother the moon.
We will find it nestled among the roots,
In a crowd of friends,
A child with a quarter face.
Stepping forward, it will offer us
A gift wrapped in moss—
A pale cone we'll use to prick our palms,
And watch as the first seeds of blood
Trickle and combine into pools,
Rich seas the roots curl and slide for.

White Out

Here on this ridge
The only color
Left is you,
And soon you too will fade.
The spruce have long
Returned to birch,
And the birch
Are quietly
Turning to snow.

Owls

Owls glide off the thin
Wrists of the night,
And using snow for their feathers
Drift down on either side
Of the wind.

I spot them
As I camp along the ridge,
Glistening over the stream beds,
Their eyes small rooms
Lit by stone lamps.

Great Bear

I always see him rolling
Slowly on his side,
Always drifting
Downwind with the moon—
A bank of soft darkness,
An old weathered dirigible
Floating low over the spruce
Toward the distant muskegs
Where the milkweed
Burst like lights on a wet
Deserted airstrip.

Hermitage

If you follow this path back
you come to a clearing
where the grass
is dark and delicate
a place so damp
it is like stepping
into something coolly interior
a land where doors open
one by one
and the wicks
of the skunk flower
burn all night over shallow pools.

Trans-Canada

At this speed our origins are groundless.
We are nearing the eve of a great festival,
The festival of wind.
Already you can see this road weakening.
Soon it will breathe
And lift away to dry its feathers in the air.
On both sides the fields of rapeseed and sunflowers
Are revolting against rows.
Soon they will scatter wildly like pheasants.
Now is the time, my friend, to test our souls.
We must let them forage for themselves,
But first—unbuckle your skin.
Out here in the darkness
Between two shimmering cities,
We have, perhaps for the last time, chance
Neither to be shut nor open, but to let
Our souls speak and carry our bodies like capes.

End

At the end of the open road we come to ourselves

Louis Simpson

All right, Louis
                 we're here
We're here at the end of the open road,
At the end of our ellipsis.

A wind and slight drizzle hide
Any other footprints.
They curl the road
Around our feet,
Sweeping it back into itself.

Louis, here in the dark we think
We see trees, giant sequoias
That break around an open marsh,
And are compelled to give them green,
A hard mossy bark, rain dripping
From their leaves.

Listen.   A bullfrog's call.
Smell the wet calm in the air.

We wait for the moon,
For the song of a white bird.

Any backdrop
    of light.

II

At Betharram

Here a mile down at Betharram
The grottos start winding
Through the earth.
The walls seep
With last year's rain,
And I go down, alone, breathing
An air that's never
Been breathed.
And the farther I go
The more I want it like this in the end—
The earth empty,
My lantern going out in the cold,
The stalactites burning
Like huge wet roots
In the dark.
There's a calm here at Betharram
Deeper than I have known.
And down this far
The heart slows and beats
As calmly as the water
That never stops,
That I hear

Far down in the caves,
Dripping for miles through stone.

The Northern Edge at Douz

Here on the northern edge
of these great sand
and salt flats,
half the night is gone
and those of us gathered
in the heat and
dead calm at Douz
are waiting for the one
bus to take us out
the way we came—
the young Garde Nationale
who for three days
has stared at the sand
in his beer, the old man
who was here for Rommel
and who'll be here
when little Said drives
his goats up the dry riverbed,
bringing word from the sand
and Four Winds, from
the salt that is boiled
and rinsed, that will

burn like tears down
the length of his face.
Here in Douz the only
star up is the one
bulb hanging by its wires
in the empty doorway,
casting light on the black
lamb that was drained
at dusk in the schoolyard,
its warm throat slit
for all of us
who wait this night out,
and are too tired
to talk the long dawn
from coming on, to stop
the lamb from bleeding, unable
to catch the blood
before it cools
and is mistaken for rain.

The Bombing of Dresden

It was the night of Fasching,
And those crossing
The Marienbrücke
Saw the cold drizzle
And the black winter sky
Suddenly ignite
Into summer.
And for an hour
The pipes in every cellar
Dripped and ran dry,
Glass doorknobs
Flowered into jewels,
And the grapes
That were left out
To smolder on their vines
Burst into stones.
For an hour
The earth was a jar,
And every beet and potato inside
Began to bleed.
The next morning
Those gathered along the Elbe

Saw the cold smoke
Of a blossom
And couldn't be sure
That it was dawn,
That what they saw
Was the sun striking a fish
And the singed weaving
Of its gills.
And nothing was left
But the snails
Gripping the dry
Walls of the cisterns,
The snails that overnight
Turned into limestone
To survive.

At the Olive Grove of the Resistance

He says that home is here,
Here where the earth falls apart
In our hands, and he points
To the one good eye they left him.
Half his world cut out, half
Buried here in the charred roots
Of his three olive trees, four fingers
Down where they made him go
On his knees, his face sliced
To the bone; left him here
To look up and see his oxen
Riding a crown of blood
Into the hills, his trees
Burning, each small olive
Turning into light; left him
To stumble back up the hill
To find his son face-down
On the stone pathway, his wife
In the shed sprawled on bags
Of seed, her white breasts
Bruised; left him to wander
Each night in the wind

Born in these black branches,
Or to stand in his small
Stone room spreading the olives
Like jewels in the sink.
And he tells me the good ones
Go north so he can pay
For the luxury of this light,
The one bare bulb that's
The only flower of his house.
And because I have come here
To listen, he cuts one open
And shows me its hard oily pit,
A small black stone wet
With light, drying in the wind
Born in his three olive trees.

On the Day of Bulls

for Philippe,
shot in the Basque riots,
Pamplona, 1978

4:30 a.m., the room quiet,
And I have made it
Longer through the night
Than the streetlight
That flickered
And died
In the courtyard.
In another hour it'll be dawn
And already too late
To ask anything
Of the day,
Of this rain beating
Against the flat
Slate roofs
Of this city.
Nine floors below
On the Boulevard Ornano,
The fruit and vegetable stalls
Stand beside the small
Iron scales tipped
All night by the rain,
The burning leaves

Of the eucalyptus
Wait to strike
The earth and go out.
I think of the bullet
You write about,
And how it lies there
Snug as a seed
Against your spine;
Of the police in Pamplona
Who'll wake on this day
To find the rain
Beating down
Out of a black sky,
Rain that's fallen all night
To cool the sores
Of the dying,
Rain that will never once
Let the dead forget
What it's like
To live on this earth.
And finally of you
Having to live out this night

Blessed by your own sweat,
Unable to flex
Your toes
Or feel the muscles
That went soft as a child's,
How only now in the last
Hour before sunrise
Can you love
This earth,
Its deep stillness,
And the way another day
Comes on without pain.

Sainte-Foy

Up in the Pyrenees they killed
Their animals with stones,
And before that
By running their herds
Into the blazing air of these foothills.
Here at the church of Sainte-Foy,
The blood of those animals
Comes back night after night.
It comes back as dust
On the old stonecutter,
The Basque who climbs every sundown
Up the long rocky path.
It comes back as earth and stone,
As hard chunks of mortar
And clay I pull from the walls
And smell what is Sainte-Foy,
A silence so deep I could stay here
And breathe this cold forever,
All this wet uncut stone
That is Sainte-Foy—
A vow I take deep, and break
As my headlights go on,

And see in the graveyard out back,
Snout buried in mud and clay,
A hog big enough for slaughter,
A loose sow that grunts once
At my lights, and doesn't move.
She stands there as I turn,
Her ears and pink back steaming
In the cold, feeding on the dead
And what dead push up.

Waiting for Trains at Col d'Aubisque

4 a.m. and rain since dark, rain dropping
From the slate roofs onto the stone walkway,
And all of us here—
The middle-aged mother and the child,
The three privates smoking
As only those going off
For good can smoke—
All of us standing at these windows,
Except the young boy out under the archway
Who has brought his father's coffin
Down out of these bare hills,
A small sheepherder's boy
Who doesn't care how old the night gets
Or how long this rain takes hold,
Only that his wool coat
Is folded neatly, and that his head rests
Over his father's shoulder,
For if this boy, this young dark-eyed Basque
From Col d'Aubisque
Whose skin will never again feel as wet
Or as wanted as it is
By all this rain,

If this small boy would talk
He would say we've stood all night
At these windows for nothing,
And that even if the morning comes
And we step out into the cold light,
Finding the world no better or worse
And ourselves still wanting
To be filled with its presence,
The words we've waited all night to say
We will have to turn into breath
And use to warm our hands.

At the Blessing of the Children in Lourdes, Winter Solstice

They never imagined it would be like this—
The gurneys suddenly slipping away,
The braces all unclasping like hands.
And then the wading out, arm in arm,
Into the waters, the ghostly flowering
Of the night clothes. And for a moment
You can see them, out in the long columns
Of light, turning like white pinwheels
In the rain, the night so cold there's just
Their breath starting its long climb
Into the sky. And scattered there
In the smoke, the crutches shining
Like wingbones, the empty fleets
Of wheelchairs all overturned,
Their wheels spinning on their starlit hubs.

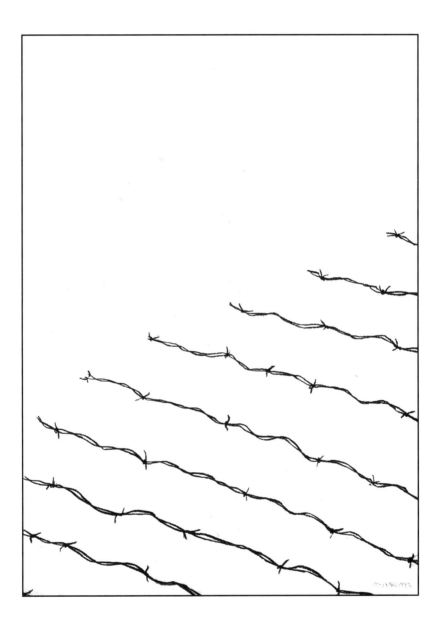

III

Selected Translations of Rolf Jacobsen

Night Music

The constellations will change,
the Big Dipper's handle
will be pulled to the south
and Orion lose his sword
before the last pain is gone,
says the stone.

I too
am allotted my share.
As the fountain's glittering dust
springs up and falls back into itself,
all my days come from somewhere inside me,
doled out in a bowl of stone.

There's a calm light around old trees.
They let the wind flow through their leaves
and stars pass high over their crowns
in majestic procession.

The Fly in the Telescope

It happened that a fly got into the telescope,
like a thorn in eternity's eye
one night when Sirius was high overhead,

and dazzled the astronomer to tears
when he saw the dark hole in the heavens
like a fist of nothing
driven through nothing.

Where is the arm that can hold me fast
and the power that can free my soul from death,
— Oh, Mr. Cembalo, come here, will you,
something has happened to the Universe! —

Until the fly saw fit to relieve itself
in the constellation of the Swan,
between the wild sun Deneb
and the shimmering flecks of Cepheus
that can only be seen in great telescopes.
Deo Gloria.

Dies Illae

The sky's great swarm of stars will circle your feet like jewels, Lord,
and the mountains lie before you as thresholds,
that day when all things are released from their laws,
when the birds are merely a song, and the waterfall a white light
and forest and ocean and sleep are one thing: deep music.
That day when those birds of passage—human hearts—
return to their forgotten May.

What will you say to me then, God Zebaot:
Be a lump of clay on the road
or, Be a flower in my forest?

Odda

The smoke rises from the earth
and climbs with its ropes into the sky
and hangs them there like antennas
that signal day and night:

We greet you, all volcanoes on earth:
Vesuvius, Birmingham, Pittsburgh, Essen.
The fire that feeds on the shadows,
that spreads through the dark from land to land,
sends its smoke into the sky
here and there:
Vesuvius, Pittsburgh, Essen.
—Let us stand
as columns of clouds in the day,
at night as fiery pillars
over Israel.

The Morning Paper

The morning paper unfolds on the 7:35 commuter
and suddenly gives all the men white wings.
They fly off in space inside the coach
with strange stiff faces
—a procession behind glass
as if to an exclusive private funeral on a star.

The Buses Long To Go Home

The buses long to go home.
They wait here in line at the terminal and long to go home
to Lualalambo, N'Kangsamba, and to Calabar,
and to the flamingo's cry at dusk.

For when it rains in the streets
it rains too in Lualalambo, N'Kangsamba, and in Calabar,
not on umbrellas but on
the long-legged stork, and on the female hippos
under the pepper trees.

When they come waddling through the flooded streets,
plastered with wet mud,
they are happy, but it has to be
a tepid rain, cool and gurgling,
streaming down the windows with reflections
of Lualalambo, N'Kangsamba, and of Calabar,
and female hippos sleeping under pepper trees.

Play

This poem will just be itself.
For I have hung a spider web all through the woods here,
and I know it will be gone by tonight, tonight
when I go to take it down again.

I wander from twig to twig and hang threads thinner than smoke.
And already today I can pass right through them.
The woods have drunk them up
and the sunshine is licking its lips.

In Countries Where The Light Has Another Color

In countries where the light has another color
the faces along the streets at dusk
can turn to pearls in a slow sea of indigo.

And you must ask yourself—what do these
fiery diadems reflect here, and whose hands
have scattered them across these dark waters?

Moss, Rust and Moths

Moss rises out of the earth.
Quiet as bats at night
it settles on the stones and waits,
or down in the grass
with ashen wings.

Rust passes from bolt to bolt
and from iron slab to iron slab in the dark,
and closely examines
if the time is right.
When the pistons have come to rest,
when the girders have gone deep into the night,
it will do its quiet, bloody work.

The stars like white moths
cluster at the dark windowpanes of heaven
and stare
and stare at the city lights.

Antenna-Forest

Up on the city's roofs are great plains.
The silence crawled there when no room was left for it
     on the streets.
Now the forest follows.
It has to be where the silence lives.
Tree after tree in strange groves.
They can barely manage since the floor is too hard.
It's a sparse forest, one branch to the east
and one to the west. Until it resembles crosses. A forest
of crosses. And the wind asks
—Who rests here
in these deep graves?

But We Live —

—But we live
through supermarkets and racks full of cheese, and we live
under the vapor trails of jets in the golden month of May
and in smoke-dimmed cities,
and we live with coughing carburetors and slamming car doors.
We live
through the TV-evening in our golden century,
on asphalt, behind tabloids and at gas stations.
We live
as statistics and as registration numbers in election years.
We live with a flower in the window,
in spite of everything we live under
hydrogen bombs the threats
of nuclear extermination, sleep-
less we live
side by side with the hungry who
die by the millions, live
with a weariness to our thoughts, live
still, live
magically inexplicably live,
live
on a star.

The Art of Flying

One great whoosh and we part from the earth oh no
everything rises at a slant like the decks of a ship,
down sail our childhood the gateway summer crushes
swept into a drawer to be saved for the next book of Moses.

O, we are wind and clouds and goodbye to Bjordammen,
far below Sinbad the Sailor and Odysseus,
Columbus, Amundsen with his frozen whiskers
drives his sled dogs across the polar ice,
you light a cigarette over the fields of Bethlehem.
Put it out over Calvary it doesn't matter,
the stewardess comes smiling with a new pack.

Fasten your seatbelts Signori—a city down there
comes sailing up in the dark like an ocean liner,
with parties on every deck and the faint
red glow of a thousand restaurants
but what should we do with the blue-black sky, now silent—
the weariness in the backs of our minds and the emptiness
    between the stars
—We came here so suddenly and suddenly
we are alone.

IV

Tornado

Four farms over it looked like a braid of black hemp
I could pull and make the whole sky ring.
And I remember there falling to earth that night
The broken slats of a barn, baling wire, straw and hay,
And one black leather Bible with a broken spine.

I think of the bulls my father slaughtered every August,
How he would pull out of that rank sea
A pair of collapsed lungs, stomach,
Eight bushels of twisted rope he called intestines,
And one bucket of parts he could never name.

In the dream that keeps circling back in the shape
Of a barn, my father has just drained
His last bull. Outside it is raining harder
Than I've ever seen, and the sky is about to step down
On one leg. And all through the barn,
As high as the loft, the smell of blood and hay.
All night, as long as the dream holds,
He keeps turning the thick slab of soap over and over,
Building the lather up like clouds in his hands.

The Wreck of the Great Northern

Where the Great Northern plunged in
The river boiled with light, and we all stood
In the tall grass staring at a tangle
Of track, and four orange coaches
And one Pullman lying under the current,
Turning the current clear. We stood staring
As though it had been there all along
And was suddenly thrust up out of the weeds
That night as a blessing, as a long sleek hallway
Dropping off into fields we'd never seen,
Into the pastures of some great god
Who sent back our steers too heavy to move,
All bloated and with green seaweed strung down
Their horns. And we all looked down
Into the lit cars at businessmen
And wives, already back to breathing water,
And saw in the cold clear tanks of the Pullman
A small child the size of my son, a porter's
White jacket, a nylon floating gracefully
As an eel.
              What the train and the river
Were saying, no one could understand.

We just stood there, breathing what was left
Of the night. How still the cars were,
How sleek, shimmering through the undertow.
And I saw the trees around us blossomed out,
The wind had come back and was blowing
Through the tall empty grass, through the high
Grain fields, the wind was rattling
The dry husks of corn.

Houdini

There is a river under this poem.
It flows blue and icy
And carries these lines down the page.
Somewhere beneath its surface
Lying chained to the silt
Harry holds his breath
And slowly files
His fingernails into moons.
He wonders who still waits at the dock
If the breasts of those young girls
Have developed since he sank.
He thinks of his parents
Of listening to the tumblers
Of his mother's womb
Of escaping upward out of puberty
Out of the pupils in his father's eyes
And those hot Wisconsin fields.
He dreams of escaping
From this poem
Of cracking the combinations
To his own body
And those warm young safes

Of every girl on the dock.
Jiggling his chains
Harry scares a carp that circles
And nibbles at his feet.
He feels the blue rush of the current
Sweeping across his body
Stripping his chains of their rust
Until each link softens
And glows like a tiny eel.
And Harry decides to ascend.
He slips with the water
Through his chains
And climbing over and over
His own air bubbles
He waves to the fish
To his chains glittering
And squirming in the silt.
He pauses to pick a bouquet
Of seaweed for the young girls
On the dock. Rising
He bursts the surface of this poem.
He listens for shouts.

He hears only the night
And a buoy sloshing in the blue.

Sloughing

for George

Back here in the bottomlands
The sloughs lie flat
As hides, breathing quietly
Among dead trees
And reeds. It is June,
Almost fifteen years
Since we stripped
And waded into those warm
Lungs, drifting among turtles
And sunfish, in what was dying
Or dead, or having to grow
Simple to survive.
You stood there knee-deep
In the smoke off the water,
Naked and wet with algae,
The old rotted shell
You'd found lifted up
Into the cold light
Like a horn, a white strand
Of fish eggs strung down
Dripping from your neck like seeds.

Tanner's Creek

All I know is what I was told:
Swim there and you die.
There was down
By the local landfill
Where the tanners dumped their sludge.
Glowing, nearly iridescent,
It bubbled, even belched,
And once I remember
Overflowed,
Roiling in our flowers
And flowerbeds,
And not even frogs would go near.
And the tanners—
On summer nights they'd gather
Under the floodlights
In the parking lot,
Or back behind the old abandoned spur,
Smoking and talking low
In the shadows
Of the empty cattle cars,
Big coarse men
In long leather aprons,

And gloves
That swallowed half the arm.

Rattlesnake Bluff

That night the lack of rain brought them
Down off the bluff,
All we saw was the grass
Fluttering where we'd burned,
And occasionally in the hot flashes
Of light, a long body stretched out off the porch
Shimmering in the dew. The next morning
When we found the hens dead
In the yard, the froth
On the cow's udder,
The skin wrapped like jewelry
Around the cold jars of preserves,
You loaded the gun and we climbed halfway up
The huge slope, leading each other around
Until we found one
As thick as our wrists,
So sluggish it could only dive once
And miss. When you pulled
And its head flew off like a bottle cap,
What little water the earth had given up
Was only good for cooling
Our hands, for wiping
The long blade after the rattles were loose.

Pollen

For weeks it was our weather,
clouding the air for days,
a fine bright storm that billowed
over barns and feedlots,
making all the livestock shine,
the horses one color.
And like luck I wanted it to last,
to have it there each morning
when I milked, the stalls
and stanchions shining,
the udders all dusted with light.

Bells

for M.L., killed in Viet Nam

I remember it was 1965, the summer
      I was put in charge
           of the bells. Above me
and high up, they waited
      like thunderheads at the top
           of the First Presbyterian Church.
And so each Sunday I would pull,
      and down out of that dark
           ringing would fall,
like flecks of glittering mica,
      dead moths, flies, and the small
           luminous bones of bats.
But most of all it was dust.
      And all summer with the sun
           high in its arc,
and the heat building slowly
      by degrees, I rose, lifted
           by that long bell rope,
and, swinging there, would pull
      the dust down, like light,
           over the bowed and sleeping Bibles.

Tornado

On Saturdays we chose Lyle
catcher for both sides.
He was one of the slow ones
and was around only
to lob the balls back,
or to chase our long flies
into the graveyard
behind Our Lady of the Fields.
The night it came sweeping down,
long, dark, a root dropping
as low as any crop duster,
we were under the pews,
everyone but Lyle,
and could tell it touched close
by the way the long
bell rope danced.
We were only nine,
and hid there
until the calm came back,
until everything began to steam—
the fields, the gravestones,
the cracked trough

of holy water—
even the fish Lyle paraded
around the infield,
the fat gray carp he said
had come swimming down
out of the clouds.
Perhaps it was the way
he was breathing,
or how he held it up
to show the blood
on its gills,
that made us all believe
he had caught it over home plate,
right where he had lost
so many in the sun.

Tornado

The last time any of us saw Gustafson's prize sow
She was rising over the floodlights
Of the poultry barns, pedalling off into a sky
Dark with wreckage.

                         If ever a sow was beautiful
It was she—1200 pounds of blue-ribbon pork
Rooted down deep in her wallow, her whole body
Lit with gold chaff.

                     By morning she was famous.
And when we found Gustafson, he was rocking
In the middle of his pigsty,
Staring west toward the county line.
And all we could hear was the rain
And its thin ticking against the leaves,
The empty swill pail still vibrating in his hands.

Tornado

for my father

Wherever he was, he was holding
the dark brim of his hat.
He was thinking of the pole sitters,
at sixty feet the shadows
of their long poles
reaching out in absurd proportions,
at sixty feet the whole county
as flat as a dance floor.
Outside shirts galloped on the lines,
the trees were breaking stride.
Far off a silo uncoiled
into the clouds, a barn knelt,
a sow quietly rose from her sty.
Then the song on the radio died.
He thought of the ballroom,
and the couples dancing
around and around for days.
By then the drift of the sitters
was so lovely he could see them all—
high on their stems, swaying
in long circles over the farmlands.
It was 1930, a Saturday, the whole sky

was darkening with wreckage.
Wherever he was, was an entrance.
He was holding the dark brim
of his hat as if tipping it.

Eclipse

Father
I have come back
To this squat Minnesota town

This shrinking house
These bald fall rooms
To find you in a stack

Of dim photos
Curled like leaves
In the back of a drawer

I run my thumb
Over your face
And feel the glassy

Bristles of your mustache
The creases
Along your cheeks

We stare at each other
And I feel you
Lose your gloss

You draw me downward
Page by page
Photo by photo

Until your body is warm
And massive and my hand
Loses itself in yours

We stand on Sorin's Bluff
And watch the wind
Die in the elms

Our shadows melt
Into one another
As we squint

Through two worn negatives
At the moon sliding
Across the sun

The valley darkens
And I am left blind
Until the sun jumps

And catches the trees
Until the moon
And you father fade

And leave me
Holding these cold
Exposures

This reverse bond
From which I pull myself
Head-first

To grip the first
Warm object
I see

On Tuesdays They Open the Local Pool to the Stroke Victims

for my sons

Thank God my own father didn't have to go through this.
Or I'd be driving him here every Tuesday
So he could swim his laps
Or splash around with the others
In the shallow end. Something terrible
Has been bled out of these lives. Why else
Would they be here pulling themselves along on their sides,
Scissoring, having to prove to their middle-aged sons
They can still dance.
                      The last three days I heard water
In the cellar, the rooms below me bumping together
Like dinghies. Somewhere back in my sleep
My father splashes in the shallow end.
All these men, even
The balding ones waiting behind the chain link fence
Watching their fathers, are down there
At the bottom of the stairs.
They are all gliding like sunlight,
Like trout across the cold floors of their breeding ponds.

Hunting Agates at White Rock

All day alone and stripped to the waist,
The sweat gleaming on the hairs
Of my stomach. Two miles
South in the gravel pit
At White Rock, and there's nothing
But my own breath going out
Among these stones. Where is the tooth
My grandfather unearthed here,
The mastodon molar as big and brown
As his old gnarled fist? Or the rock
I heaved at the harmless bullsnake,
And the light burning that day
Off the stones? As a boy
I used to go silent for days,
Trying to hear how the earth sounds
To the dead, and heard the huge
Silver tumbler in the cellar
Turning the stones day and night,
Until they came out gray
With sludge and needed washing
Under the hose. Now there is nothing
But the earth at White Rock

Lying open like a grave,
With just enough light to gather
My stones. Soon the winds will come,
And the first martins flying
For the night into the bottomlands,
The heat lightning a mile out
Over the flood plain.
And the long walk up County O,
Following those three stars
That come full circle to bless
The thorn bush I darkened with blood,
And the old Baptist cemetery
Where the Swedes of White Rock
Lay down in the winter of '39,
My grandfather among them,
And found home in these stones.

The Old Liberators

Of all the people in the mornings at the mall,
It's the old liberators I like best,
Those veterans of the Bulge, Anzio, or Monte Cassino
I see lost in Automotive or back in Home Repair,
Bored among the paints and power tools.
Or the *really* old ones, the ones who are going fast,
Who keep dozing off in the little orchards
Of shade under the distant skylights.
All around, from one bright rack to another,
Their wives stride big as generals,
Their handbags bulging like ripe fruit.
They are almost all gone now,
And with them they are taking the flak
And fire storms, the names of the old bombing runs.
Each day a little more of their memory goes out,
Darkens the way a house darkens,
Its rooms quietly filling with evening,
Until nothing but the wind lifts the lace curtains,
The wind bearing through the empty rooms
The rich far off scent of gardens
Where just now, this morning,
Light is falling on the wild philodendrons.

Tornado

I had seen Ferris wheels before, but this one
Was as tall as a silo. And nights I could see it
Turning over Drabowski's barn, its gondolas
Rocking in the bright confusion of stars.
That night the tornado came sashaying
Over the farmlands, its dark hemline dragging up
Trees, dust, mile after mile of gleaming fence line,
All you could hear were those long guy-wires
Vibrating through the rain, a hum so deep
That farmers all over the county looked up
From their evening chores, women moved
Toward open windows, expecting to find the stars.
And even outfielders forgot for a moment
The words of the anthem, turned, and with ballcaps
Over their hearts, looked up at the long arc
Of the sky, could see it through the driving rain,
Grinding in the middle of Drabowski's field,
Its huge ghostly outline looming over the barns.
And some small boy at the top, rocking
In the wreckage, his face through the rain
Looking down from those intricate spokes of light.

About Rolf Jacobsen

Rolf Jacobsen was born in 1907 and lived much of his adult life in Hamar, a town north of Oslo, Norway, where he worked as a journalist and newspaper editor. Widely recognized as one of the great Scandinavian poets of the twentieth century, he published numerous volumes of poetry and played a critical role in the introduction of modernism to Norwegian poetry. A member of the Norwegian Academy of Language and Literature, he was honored with many prizes and awards for his work, including the Norwegian Critics' Prize, the Aschehoug Prize, and both the Dobloug Prize and the Grand Nordic Prize from the Swedish Academy. His poetry has been translated into more than twenty languages. Rolf Jacobsen died in 1994.

The poems in this collection have been selected from the following volumes: from *Vrimmel*: "Odda" and "Moss, Rust and Moths"; from *Fjerntog*: "Dies Illae"; from *Hemmelig liv*: "The Fly in the Telescope," "Play," and "Night Music"; from *Sommeren i gresset*: "The Buses Long To Go Home" and "In Countries Where The Light Has Another Color"; from *Stillheten efterpå*: "The Morning Paper"; from *Headlines*: "The Art of Flying" and "But We Live—"; from *Pusteøvelse*: "Antenna-Forest." All are published in Oslo, Norway, by Gyldendal Norsk Forlag.

About the Author

Robert Hedin was born and raised in Red Wing, Minnesota, and holds degrees from Luther College and the University of Alaska. He has taught at Sheldon Jackson College in Sitka, Alaska, the Anchorage and Fairbanks campuses of the University of Alaska, the University of Minnesota, and Wake Forest University in Winston-Salem, North Carolina, where he served as Poet-in-Residence for a number of years. Awards for his work include three Creative Writing Fellowships from the National Endowment for the Arts, a Bush Foundation Artist Fellowship, a Minnesota State Arts Board Fellowship, a North Carolina Arts Council Fellowship, the 1988 *Nebraska Review* Prize in Poetry, and a 1980 New York Poetry in Public Places Award from the New York State Arts Council. He lives in Frontenac, Minnesota, with his wife, Carolyn, and their two children.